WITH A
FULL
Heart

*Verses to Ignite Your Faith
and Feed Your Soul*

A POETRY COLLECTION BY
WALKER STRADLEY

WITH A FULL HEART
Verses to Ignite Your Faith and Feed Your Soul

Copyright © 2022 Walker Stradley

ISBN: 979-8-9857704-3-8

Book Design by
Transcendent Publishing

TRANSCENDENT
publishing

Printed in the United States of America.

This book is for all my grandkids – Emily, Stryker, Gavin, Amelia, Savannah, Adelynn, Mason, Case and Jake. Life is hard at times; in those times, accept the challenge. More importantly, life is a beautiful gift, so always be grateful, stay humble, and remember:

As we seek lofty things

We may never fly

With small earthly wings

We will try, we will try!

I love you all.

CONTENTS

1 Corinthians 2:9

However, as it is written: "What no eye has seen, what no ear has heard, and what no human mind has conceived" – the things God has prepared for those who love him…"

Step 11 of AA states: "Sought through prayer and meditation to improve our conscious contact with God as we understood Him, praying only for knowledge of His will for us and the power to carry that out."

My words in this book reflect on how I personally understand our Creator. My life has gone full circle and I have been given a second chance at living, one little precious day at a time. I don't seek Him like I should but I focus on what is beautiful today... because of the God of my understanding. If you read this, God bless you and have a wonderful day!

INTRODUCTION

What do a love of booze, a love of food, and a love of words have in common? For me, it turns out, quite a bit. The first two, which I loved to excess for much of life, tried to steal my joy, and the third one helped give it back to me. I have always loved life – in many ways too much – a trait inherited from my grandfather. His loves were fishing and hunting and drinking, not necessarily in that order. I couldn't bait a hook or shoot straight if my life depended on it, but when it came to the drinking I did better than most.

I gave up the booze for good on September 8, 1992, but what I soon learned is that addiction is a sneaky thing, often moving from one drug to another in an attempt to maintain control. In my case that next drug was food (or, more accurately, sugar- and chemical-laden substances masquerading as such), and by my one-year sobriety anniversary I tipped the scales at three-hundred and nine pounds and was wearing size fifty-four pants. I was miserable at this weight; I also knew that continuing along this path would end things as surely as the bottle. Dr Bob and Bill W.'s "Big Book" had showed me a blueprint for a sober life, but now I needed help in navigating this new challenge. In 2002, that help showed up in the form of David Greenwalt, who I met when I googled his online supplement store. I was looking for protein powder that was recommended for a diet, the latest in a series I had tried that had led nowhere except back to the fridge or cupboard.

One day I found myself on Greenwalt's website and saw that he offered a twelve-week "body transformation" course. Did I believe it? I wasn't sure, but what (other than about a hundred pounds) did I have to lose? I signed up for his course and did quite well, achieving significant and what I hoped was sustainable weight loss; later I attended his school that teaches major aspects of living a healthy life, including exercise, nutrition, and what I needed most: *emotional* sobriety. Thanks to his teachings and our one-on-one work together, I still weigh one hundred ninety-five pounds today. I also consider David a mentor and a very close friend.

That said year, 2002, I wrote a silly rhyme to describe how I was feeling: a little hungry but trying to stay positive about it. When I showed it to David, he asked me if I'd ever considered putting my thoughts into poems instead of obsessing about what kind of delicious, unhealthy treats I might find in the kitchen. That's when I started writing poems on a regular basis. They have become my "journal" of sorts, chronicling my growth in certain areas of my life. They are poems of friends, family, love for my wife and kids and nature... and, most importantly, my love of my Creator and gratitude for every day's sunset that brings me closer to our meeting. Not that my journey is over – far from it – and I continue to enjoy new experiences and observe, fascinated, how some areas of my life have come full circle. I hope as you read this book you are inspired to live life to the fullest, to keep looking for your dreams and to do the work required to make those dreams come true. I pray you seize and cherish each moment, and that we will meet one day, either here or in eternity as we trudge the happy road of destiny together.

A New Compass

I'm moving in the wrong direction
That much I can see
It's time to make a correction
Ah yes, it's up to me!

I'm sick of this road I'm walking
It's really just a dead end
I'm tired of the way I'm traveling
So I'm gonna start a new road, my friend

I'm mixing up some mortar
I'm working on a brick at a time
I'm building me a new road
It's gonna travel just fine

Yes, I'm building me a new road
I'm working with all my heart
I'm gonna travel a million miles
One step is where I'll start

A Farmer's Field

There was a rock in a farmer's field.
It increased his labor and hurt his yield.
Then he decided one sunny day
To seriously move the rock away!
Ready to strain, prepared to toil,
It easily moved from fertile soil.
Crops had been lost from previous years,
All because of the farmer's fears.
Now he smiled and wondered why?
All he had to do...was TRY!!!

A Man of Sorrows

A man of many sorrows,
on Earth He had no home
A few tried to follow Him,
but for the most part He was a man alone.

A gift the world rejected
as it was meant to be
Majesty perfected,
a personal king for me.

I once was lost and weary,
my soul not near complete
That man alone did find me,
we had a chance to meet.

He became my shepherd,
for I am just a lamb
Through love he took my sorrows,
thank God for the great I Am

Amen

My Best Friend

My best friend, as the saying goes,
is black and furry and he's got a wet nose.
He listens to me like he understands.
Where is that trait in our fellow man?

It does not matter what mood I'm in,
he's happy to see me again and again.
Just a rub or a touch suits him fine.
He's there for me if I've got the time!

He doesn't care what I look like,
the color of my skin,
never judges my demeanor,
regardless of the mood I'm in.

Ready to play at the toss of a ball
or for a leisurely walk,
he doesn't understand every word I say,
but really listens when I talk!

Ready to fight to the death to keep me
from any harm,
he looks up at me with caring and trust,
he really is my best friend
here on the farm!

If I could describe this four-legged friend,
it's hard to know where to start.
Caring, compassionate, loves without end ...
God help me be like my dog,
with his unconditional heart!

A Prayer

Lord God,

Make us into a vessel,
a river of honor and light
Allow us to be a beacon
to a lost soul's darkest night

Give us the strength and the courage
to always remember Your word
Allow us to shout from the mountain
to all who never have heard

Let all gladly carry other's burdens
without as much as a sound
And through this, oh precious savior
One more believer is found

Thank you, Lord, bless all who are here
Bless those who are gone,
for their spirits are near
We wait for our King,
our shepherd, our savior
And if Christ comes today,
may we be found in His favor

And if not today,
we will wait for Your time
His will always be done,
never mine, never mine

Amen

A Bird and its Beauty

I gazed upon some birds a-bathing.
So beautiful to see.
God's creation, so amazing,
nature's gift for you and me!

And as my feathered friends were splashing
in the water all around,
A song so sweet above the chirping,
a most amazing sound.

Sweet melody so magical,
a wonder to be heard
Hidden treasures in all of God's creation,
The beauty of a bird!

A Priceless Gift

A priceless gift He gives to you,
His beautiful chosen one
No heart can understand His love
that gave His only Son!
How can I accept this joy,
I don't deserve this prize
For I am a dark and lowly sinner
and, yes, I realize

A sinless lamb, He died for me,
He died for every man
I try in vain yet cannot see,
I don't fully understand
My sorrows, my fears and every wasted thing,
all the shame I've done
A priceless gift He gives to you,
His beautiful chosen one

No eye has seen, no ear has heard,
no mind can understand
What waits on high, a Golden secret for
the brotherhood of man!
So on my knees I give Him thanks,
my soul awakes when done
A priceless gift He gives to you,
His beautiful chosen one.

A Servant, a King

My pride is a thorn,
I'm often unwise
My ship, lost and sinking at sea
Oh remove the thorn's sting
and give praise to my King
He died on the cross just for me!

A vessel slowly sinking in a furious storm,
The squall had made sailors its slaves
Oh such a thing, to sail with a King
For he calmed the wind and the waves

A donkey colt never ridden
Never rode by one single man
Oh such a thing, to carry a King
Bridled by Jesus's sweet hand!

A man of sorrows, rejected by all
God's Lamb with no imperfection
Oh such a thing, a crucified King
We live through Christ's resurrection!

His glory is stronger when we are weak
God's love endures till the end
What a beautiful thing to walk with the King
In Christ, we all have a friend!

And So it Seems

And so it seems, just us two
and this cozy little room,
Nothing really on my mind
but the smell of your perfume.
We can sit and talk a bit or see what's on TV.
Anything you want to do,
I'm just glad you're here with me.

I see your face and hear your voice
yet much to my surprise
The only thing that interests me
is the color of your eyes.
I swear it's true, that me and you
should be used to us by now,
Yet darling when you hold my hand
I'm trembling somehow.

And so it seems, it's just us two,
it doesn't matter where we are.
Wishes really do come true,
for I wished upon a star!
God was shining down on me
and made my wish come true!
And so it seems, my beautiful Dream,
God – He gave me you!
I love you

Abba

Sometimes my soul gets weary,
I don't have what life demands
So today I went to my Father,
He alone who understands
I spoke of all my troubles,
as tears rolled down my face
The last thought I remember...
I need Your mercy and grace

I've known so many joys in life,
blessings too many to count
Yet sometimes life feels like a living hell
as problems start to mount
So today in a secret hideaway
I cried out in pain
I thought of all the mistakes I've made
as I held my head in shame

Today I spoke with my Father
as He listened tenderly
And as the tears filled my eyes
He put His hand on me
A peace and calm came over me
as I wiped away the tears
I felt new strength within my soul
as worries disappeared

Today I looked for my Father,
the One who sits on high
In times like these it's He alone
who won't judge me when I cry
And I walked away from my garden
I felt my strength return
For all my years here on Earth,
the one thing I may have learned:

Always seek your Father,
the one that's yours alone
Seek Him when you're troubled
and you feel you're on your own
Tell Him of your burdens
as you sit in a secret place
Let all your strength be restored
from tender mercy and redeeming grace.

Amen

A Simple Wooden Pew

I sit without hesitation
on this simple wooden pew
Back again to say amen
and do what sinners do
In all things there lies a lesson
if I let myself be taught
Sitting on that old piece of wood there's
a gift that can't be bought

The gifts that I've been given,
as far back as I remember
Celebrations, this or that,
every Christmas in December
I've kept a few, I've lost some too,
some have broke or been outgrown
I'm blessed with the gift of a worn-out pew
and it feels just like a throne

I sit with jubilation
on a simple wooden pew
I gaze outside the windowpane,
springtime comes into view
Thank you, Lord, for all your gifts,
most of them I never see
Thank you for this wooden pew
and the love You've given me.

Athletic Christmas

'Twas the night before Christmas
when all through the land
Those with a vision were making a plan!
Ideas full of action with sweat and devotion
A great thing of beauty when put into motion!

While some stay asleep in their beds as they choose
The other elites are lacing their shoes!
With you in your warm-ups and I in mine too
We head out to the track…(a gym will also do!)

On runners, on swimmers, on climbers and hikers
Lifters, crossfitters, skaters and bikers
To the end of the pool! To the top of the wall!
Swim away, climb away, sweat away all!

They were all lean and fit, or well on their way
Putting exercise plans in action today
Their eyes had a twinkle, they had sweat on their
brow
No waiting for New Year's, they live for the now!

Some on their own, others on teams
Humble and grateful, fulfilling their dreams
Dreams of achievement for these stellar few
Shhh! Hey listen! They're calling to you!

Come, won't you join us?
We'll have a ball!
The best holiday ever,
MERRY CHRISTMAS TO ALL!

Be Still and Open Your Eyes

I took a walk down a dusty road,
the sun was just starting to rise.
When I heard a voice so loud and clear,
"Be still and open your eyes."
Well my eyes were wide open, I thought I could see
So what did I hear and were they talkin' to me?
So I stood very still, as still as could be
And then God, He opened my eyes

You see, my eyes had been closed for a very long time
I was blind to the gifts the Lord insisted were mine
So much wasted effort, so much wasted time
And then God, He opened my eyes

So as we all ramble down life's dusty roads
As we shoulder our burdens and life's heavy loads
As we carry our crosses as Christ only knows
May God open all of our eyes

Let us all be aware of the gifts God has given
Sharing our faith for a life that's worth living
May our hearts be filled with love and thanksgiving
Please God, open all of our eyes

Amen

Beautiful Friend

This time of year as seasons change
And summer gives way to fall
I, in kind, renew my mind
Counting blessings one and all

The leaves on the trees, their display
The colors seem just for me!
I hold our friendship in that special way
Colored so wonderfully

And as the evenings cool down
I take a breath and pause to comprehend
Such a splendid time in my life
For you are such a wonderful friend

Very soon it will turn colder
I look forward to winter's first snow
In my life I'm one season older
So I thought that you should know

Nature's beauty puts on her colors
It touches my heart to see
I'm reminded of our friendship
You are a beautiful friend to me!

Brave at Heart

I believe in a labor of love,
To follow your heart's desire.
To pursue lofty visions above,
When you feel you can reach no higher!

When every ounce of strength is gone,
And you know you're at the end of your rope!
When you can't imagine continuing on,
Lost with no glimmer of hope.

I believe in people!
Those that tried and failed.
For if you try, you try again,
Until your ship has sailed!

Those great among men have courage within
To venture where most never start!
Seeking and learning, the journey enduring
Brave to follow their heart!

Bread of Life

I belong to Jesus Christ,
My Lord, my shelter, the Bread of Life!
I'll never hunger I'll never thirst,
To believe in Him, to put Him first

Earthly desires, they tempt all men,
I must admit, I'm one of them
We all like sheep have gone astray
Yet all my sins are washed away!

There stands a name above all names
Whose love is greater than all my shame
He's at the door for all who knock
For just one sheep He leaves the flock

The redeemer calls to follow Him
As earthly treasures fade to dim
Oh beautiful song that resonates
Let's go to Him, the Master waits!

Broken Nation

Mighty God in heaven,
If it be Thy will
Restore our broken nation,
for we have fallen ill
Restore Your people, for here we are,
a nation so divided
We have squandered Your precious gifts,
all You have provided

Oh Lamb of God upon Your throne,
hear my heartfelt plea
Our land is now in bondage,
come and set us free
We have turned our backs on You, our God,
our Morning Star
We all, like sheep, have gone astray,
and now look at where we are

God in all Your glory, the author of Eternal Salvation
Forgive our fallen country,
restore our once great nation
Make us again United, a sweet land of liberty
Rebuild our once great nation
and let it start with me.

Amen

Cinderella Story

I'd like to share a Cinderella story,
a real-life fairytale
God's gifts in all their glory,
Adelynn and Savannah Gayle,
Two little baby birdies, snuggled into a nest of gold
Two precious little angels, not quite one month old

The Lord whispered to Adelynn,
as He sat upon His throne
Now is the time for your life to begin
and, child, you're not alone!
For I have given you a sister,
you will always be best friends
As I have blessed your family
and created you as twins!

More precious than rare diamonds,
a treasure more priceless than any gold
For God has blessed our family
and increased it by twofold!
So there is my story, my real-life fairytale…
The adventure begins for these heavenly twins,
Adelynn and Savannah Gayle.

I love you and you,
Pops

Close Your Eyes

Close your eyes, dear child be still
For by your side I'll always be
Know that I can never leave you
Remove your chains, I've set you free

Take My yoke, My yoke is easy
I believe in all that you can do
Lean on Me in times of trouble
Know that I see faith in you

Come with Me when you are weary
I have a place where you can rest
When life, at times, is dark and dreary
I'll never fail you, for you are blessed

My ways surpass your comprehension
My strength beyond all mortal men
My love is timeless without dimension
Boundless love without end

Amen

Door Hinges

May joy and peace surround you,
May love be the hinge on your door
And as for good things in your life
My wish for you is MORE!

More smiles from people you meet
More laughter in your heart
May your day be sweeter than sweet
From daylight until it's dark

And when the day is through
May love be the hinge on your door
And tomorrow as we start anew
My wish for you is MORE!

Dreams Can Come True

Some wish they could swim
but fear they might drown
They dream about flying
with their feet on the ground
You long to be stronger, some say you are weak
Dreaming and wishing are not so unique

We all have our dreams, everyone does
Millions of wishes, we wish just because
Then there are those who arise from the ashes
Grizzled and hardened from all of their crashes

Coming up short many hundreds of times
Yet breaking the chain self-bondage defines
Refusing to quit, determined to win
Obliged to keep trying, to never give in

These are the heroes I most admire
Scarred with the marks that show heart and desire
No longer silent, my soul it does scream
So reach for my hand as we follow our dream

Help me to swim, insist that I fly
Help me grow stronger, to do more than just try
I know I can do this, I can do this with you
For I see your scars that show dreams can come true

Eskimo Kiss

My grandmom came and visited today
I greeted her in my most northern way
The way people do where it's cold and it snows
I really like to kiss as do the Eskimos!

When she visits me she's my very special guest
Her love for me is the absolute best
We have a bond that's hard to describe
So we greet each other like the Eskimo tribe!

My grandmom loves me and it really shows
I love her too so we touch nose-to-nose
And when she leaves I hate to see her go
For my grandmom is my favorite Eskimo

But I won't cry, I know I'll see her again
I love my grandmom, she's my Eskimo friend

Expect the Unexpected

You might call me silly,
others will think I'm dumb
Expect the unexpected
and it will surely come

Don't ever stop the raging river
inside of you that's wild
Dare to dream unthinkable things
with the wisdom of a child

Believe in others, believe in yourself,
there's nothing you can't do
Always give a helping hand,
I'll try to do that too

Dare to dream impossible things,
take all life gives, not some
Expect the unexpected
and it will surely come!

Father Will Take Me Home

My mother brought me into this world,
my Father will take me home
Throughout the day, come what may,
I remember I'm never alone
For Christ, He stands beside me,
the Holy Spirit has me by the hand
One faithful day, I'll fly away,
my home is in the Promised Land!

At times my boat is loaded,
my troubles can put me on my knees,
Yet our loving Savior was quoted,
"In Me you may have peace."
Praise God, all forgiven sinners,
as the world is ever so demanding
Our Christ He overcame this world,
showed a peace beyond understanding

My Lord has prepared a heavenly place
and I'll go there one of these days
Every knee shall bow to His face,
every tongue will give Him praise
I love my mother, she brought me into this world,
my Father has a world without end
The circle will never be broken,
He's promised I'll be going home again!

Father God, it's Uncle Sam

Father God, it's Uncle Sam,
I hope you remember who I am
I come to you on bended knee
I once was brave I once was free

Now it seems I'm lost and confused
A nation divided by political views
I seem to have lost what once was humble
I've eroded, I'm distressed, I've started to crumble

So Lord, I pray for the American
I pray to love my fellow man
I ask dear God, let hatred cease
I'm weary and broken, I'm on my knees

I ask these things in your precious name
And though I know I have myself to blame
I pray that I may return to you
Have mercy, oh God, on the red, white and blue

Amen!

Dancing

I'll dance with you in the rain,
with you it's beautiful weather
Forever, now and again,
we'll walk through the storms together
And if ever I slip away
and God should call me home
A part of me will stay,
I shall never leave you alone
Together with you there's nothing I lack,
for you are my chosen one
I love you to the moon and back,
you are my shining sun
And when the sun sets and darkness appears,
you are the stars that shine
Darling, my dear, with all of my heart
I treasure that you are mine

Father's Day

Today is a special unique sort of day
We honor our fathers in some sort of way
Whether still living or perhaps passed away
We give them our thoughts or some words we can say

Dear Dad, I love you, I want you to know
You are the tops, as far as dads go
I think about mom, how you loved her so
You worked hard for our family and helped it to grow
Good times and hard times, you always were there
We have butted heads, you're hardheaded, I swear!
Yet you stand on your principles
that you think are fair

My conclusion, dear Dad, is you really do care
So dear, kind sir, on today of all days
You're in my thoughts in so many ways
I think you are special, it's you that I praise
I'm hopeful this verse somehow relays…
I love you.

HAPPY FATHER'S DAY

Foolish Heart

I would be a worthy captain,
I could sail a ship of fools.
If you add up all the things I've done,
countless times I've broke the rules.
I tend to forget my losses,
I exaggerate every win,
What in the world was I thinking?
Where do I even begin?
Surely all the mistakes
I've made should have taught me
a thing or two
But when it comes to my heart
I have no regrets
I'll always be a fool for you

My love, please forgive me
for all my silly ways
You are and will forever be
the sunshine of my days
And when my life is over
and my foolish ways are through
Please know I'm foolishly waiting
For I'll always be a fool for you

Forty Lashes Minus One

Forty days He fasted
Tempted to turn stones to bread
Man does not live on bread alone
Yet on God's holy word instead
Dear God, let us stay hungry
Let us always be athirst
The well of living waters
Let us always seek You first

Forty lashes minus one
My God, my savior, what have we done?
A crown of thorns that pierced Your head
Above Your crown a sign which read,
"JESUS OF NAZARETH, THE KING
OF THE JEWS"
The king of kings we did accuse
Oh precious Lamb, who could have known?
No greater love than the love You've shown

In all our ways let us run to You
Guided by faith, not our worldly view
Lead us God just for today
For in Jesus name, it's this we pray

We pray for those hungry,
We pray for the angry and the lost

We ask that we may guide them,
and bring them to the foot of the cross
For it's at the cross You meet us,
You open up the door
Every unfed sinner will hunger
and thirst no more

AMEN

Gifts from God

Love the people God gave you
We're here for just a little while
Show them what they mean to you
You can start with a simple smile
One thing to remember
As you start a brand-new day
All of our days are numbered
Soon we all must go away
Cherish the people in your life
Every single one
Imagine a day without them
For that day could very well come,
Adore the people God gave you
For time is ticking away
They belonged to God before they were yours
And He'll want them back some day

Ginny's Lamb

As time goes by I realize what a lucky man I am.
Take for instance my daughter Gin
and her beautiful little lamb.
Each day I pray just a little while,
I thank my Shepherd above.
For giving me family like Ginny
and her little lamb of love.

God above is good to me,
He's given me such a treasure.
Sons and daughters and little lambs,
such wealth one cannot measure.
So here I am, such a lucky man,
I can promise you that I am!
Take, for instance, my daughter Gin
and her beautiful little lamb.

I love you, Case,
Pops

Give to God Your All

The journey's long, yet keep on going,
give to God your all
And if your burden becomes too heavy,
He'll catch you when you fall
Christ, our lord and mighty king,
a savior for all who come
Confess your sins, invite Him in,
you'll know peace when you are done

A godly angel rolled away the stone,
I remember things such as these
In all the world's confusion, Christ,
He gives us peace
So for today, whatever it brings,
remember you're not alone
For we shall soar on majestic wings
for He rolled away the stone

Eternity, for you and me,
is just around the bend
We've traveled far and in a few more miles
We'll have reached the journey's end
The day will come, when God will call
To each and everyone
In that solemn hour we know our walk is done

The journey is long but keep on climbing
You'll reach the mountaintop
Don't give up, don't ever quit and,
if you ever want to stop
Remember once you reach the peak,
God gives a heavenly view
A mighty king, our risen savior,
He's waiting there for you

Amen

God Grew a Tree

God grew a tree from one tiny seed
For the lost and the lonely, for the sinner in need
From one simple seed placed in God's hand
Nothing could stop Him, for God had a plan

He nourished the soil with the sun and the rain
Year after year, again and again
On a hillside a cypress grew mighty and tall
Yet God had a plan, the tree was to fall

The fall of mankind led to the fall of a tree
A cross was then built for you and for me
Nailed to that cross was God's only son
And so it is finished, God's plan was done.

God took a seed and He had made up his mind
His love is eternal for all of mankind
Imagine how strong God's love has to be
From one tiny seed God grew a tree

Amen

For Ann

Your beauty, dear Ann, is timeless
In any shade at all
Bright colors of a summer day
Cool colors of the fall
Ah yes, we both grow older
And when my sight gets dimmer
The colors of your beauty remain
You'll always have that shimmer
My love for you is timeless
Though looks don't stay the same
You'll always be my beautiful friend
That can never change

Good Morning

May your joy be great, may it continue to grow
Let your cup be filled, let it overflow
With beautiful things that are precious and treasured
May your joy be great in infinite measure

May your worries be few as you sit by the fire
Just like the flames, let your spirit rise higher
Peace in your heart, I wish this for you
Beautiful spirit, may your worries be few

Work with your hands, never give in to pride
If you ever fall short remember you tried
Wherever you are, whatever you do
Seek lofty things destined for you

So as I now close this poem meant for you
Keep looking for joy in all that you do
Keep towing the line to your journey's end
And always remember, you're my beautiful friend!

Gratitude

What if today, the here and the now,
We were able to say we are grateful somehow.
What if our vision, our view twenty/twenty,
As far as complaints, we didn't have any!

To walk by a stranger and take time to smile,
To see someone lonely and talk just a while,
To pause for a moment and renew your mind,
What if we all chose to do something kind?

What if today was your best day ever,
To find some little way to make our world better,
What if this moment, right here and right now,
We were able to say we are grateful somehow

I am grateful

Greater is He

Greater is He who is in you than he who is in the world.
So come to the cross, God's venue
Let His banner be unfurled!
I sought the Lord, and he heard me,
and delivered me from all my fears,
Greater is He who is in me,
and though I've cried a river of tears.

He will wipe every tear from their eyes,
they'll be no more death or sorrow.
My soul's foundation, the cornerstone,
He is my strength for tomorrow
Just a bit longer on life's rocky mountain,
we're almost to its peak
His eyes are upon the humble,
the poor and timid and meek.

His eyes are upon the righteous,
His ears hear every cry
I am the worst among sinners,
yet for me Christ chose to die!
I will bless the Lord at all times:
His praise shall always be heard.
Greater is He who is in you
than he who is in the world.

Happiness

Happiness, it can't be bought
It's not for sale yet often sought
The newest gadget or fancy thing
A brand-new car or diamond ring
The strongest drug or finest liquor
Won't help you find it any quicker
Here's the secret, between us two
Happiness is inside of you!

Happy Easter

Who was and is and is to come
Hope for many and yet for some
Nothing more than a fairytale
To think mankind could honestly nail
A king as servant, the Lamb of God
Crucified while many applaud
For crimes that we are guilty of
Awesome wonder, eternal love

As I fall short with best-made plans
 I hit my knees and there He stands
My God, my grace on high above
Awesome wonder, eternal love

The Lord our God is risen today
We all are blessed, somehow, some way
A gift that I'm unworthy of
Awesome wonder, eternal love

Amen

He Died for You!

Are you worth dying for?
Your Savior thinks you are.
Worldly desires may have made you fall,
it matters not how far.
For He alone gave His life.
He bled and died for you.
God offered up His only son,
you might not of ever knew.
Our Lord is full of mercy,
He is full of grace
He bore your sins upon the cross,
Yes Jesus took your place.
For you are His beloved child,
you're His precious kid
He loves you so much
He would die for you
That's exactly what He did!

Amen

Hey, You're Sittin' in My Seat!

Come next Sunday I'll be right over there
So don't get MY seat, I mean it, I swear!
I know I shouldn't say that, it's a sin, you see
But that is in fact my seat and it belongs to me!

All the places I've sat down in in my life
Me, by myself, or with the pleasure of my wife
All those seats were just places to sit
That seat over there makes me spiritually fit

So come next Sunday if my soul hasn't flown away
I'll be in that seat but just let me say
If by chance you bring someone new
I'll be more than happy to share it with you

Amen

My Father's Hands

When I was a little boy
I'd reach for my father's hands
To guide me and to lead me,
and though now that I'm a man
I find myself seeking shelter,
from life's storms and worldly things
So I still reach for my father
and the shelter of his wings

I've walked down some dusty old roads,
seems like a million times or more
I long to set foot on streets made of gold
and walk by the crystal shore
So today let my feet be guided,
through faith and not by sight
As I reach for the hands of my father,
His mercy and all His might

I've walked this earth almost sixty-five years,
set aside my childish ways
Yet I long for the heart of an innocent child
so I can enter heaven some day
So I reach for my loving father,
a lingering child inside this man
Everything I long for, comes from the strength
of my Father's hands.

His Daughter

On my darkest of days
And my inadequate ways
I remember whose daughter I am
I quit feeling down
I straighten my crown
Thank God for my precious Lamb!
When I feel full of woe
There's one thing I know
It's buried deep in my heart
Though my thoughts can run wild
I'm His innocent child
He grants me a brand-new start
He's loving and kind
And while renewing my mind
I feel that this is what is to be
And between me and you
When my life is through
My spirit is eternally free

Amen

Hope and Faith and Love

Last night I dreamt of our Savior
He gently came to me
He took me by the hand and said,
"There's something I want you to see."

I looked down from a very high mountain
What treasures I did see!
Worldly kingdoms and all their splendor
All there could ever be.

And then I looked at Jesus
He tenderly touched my face,
"All you see was offered to Me
Yet on the cross I took your place."

I fell down at the feet of my Lord
I could scarcely take it in
This sad and lonely sinner
And then He touched me once again.

"I came to serve the Father,
for all criminals such as you,"
"But now you are a child of Mine
And you shall serve Him too!"

So when I awoke, I knelt to pray
And thank my God above
For showing me timeless treasures
Of hope and faith and love!

Amen

I Dream of a Christmas

I dream of a Christmas, the ground covered in snow
Children can't wait, they're wanting to know
What's in that gift under the tree!
Can we open one early? Perhaps, we will see!

I wish for a Santa, his beard flowing and white
A special reindeer named Rudolph,
his nose red and bright
Cookies and milk from the whole family
Will they be gone Christmas morning?
Perhaps, we will see!

I long for a song in this holiday hour
Sung from the spirit of a beautiful choir
I yearn for Silent Night voiced just for me
Will voices be heard? Perhaps, we will see!

I dream of a time when fighting comes to an end
Suppose for moment world peace among men
No more resentment or hostility
Would this happen one day? Perhaps, we will see!

I dream of a Christmas that's special for you
Laughter and joy in all that you do
May your holiday be more than you hoped it could be
Merry Christmas with love from the Stradley family!

I Give Things to God

Sometimes at night before I drift off in slumber
My body is weary and I'm about to go under
One thing that I do before I go off to sleep
I give things to God, things I know not to keep

I give Him my worries, the stuff I can't control
For I am His child and He has my soul
I tell Him of my journey for today's journey is done
The battles I've fought, the few I have won

The victories I give Him are His, don't you see?
For I live for Christ and Christ lives in me
And though I am tired and my eyes start to close
I know my Lord died for sinners and I'm one of those

So sometime tonight before you drift off to sleep
Take a moment to give Him the things you can't keep
Give Him your burdens, don't hold even one
For we are loved by our Father and we live through
His son

Amen

I Hold onto Amazing Grace

I hold onto amazing grace
as I rise with the Son, a new day to face
Troubles come, as they always do
yet there is power in His blood, I know that's true!
And when life's road is rough as can be,
I'm never alone, for He walks with me.
Any dismay that tomorrow may bring
is washed away because of my King
Yes, whatever life brings I won't back down!
Amazing grace, how sweet the sound

Amen

I Love You

Dear precious one, what can I say?
For my heart's overrun in a beautiful way,
Mere spoken words cannot express
The way that you move, the way that you dress
I simply must be the world's luckiest man
The way that you touch me when you hold my hand
 My heart is too full for me to convey
So precious one, all I can say,
I love you

I Saw God

I do believe I saw God,
just the other day
I felt His presence thru and thru
as I watched my grandson play!

And as I silently stood there,
there was a small bird in a nearby tree
Though it wasn't long she sang a song and God,
He spoke to me!

This, and all creation,
the innocence of a child
All this for me until eternity,
thru Christ is reconciled!

So pay attention to the things around you,
every single one
Know that they are gifts from God
and remember His risen Son
Today is a new creation, rejoice,
for the new is here!
Therefore, if anyone is in Christ, rejoice,
for our God is near!

Amen

I Wish You More

For every blessing we share in life
from the cradle to heaven's door,
Here are just a few things, of which I wish you more:

More time on your knees alone
talking to your Creator
For when you are lost and lonely,
there is no one greater

More time with the kids you love,
they're memories in the making
Backyard swings, those kind of things,
the times for picture-taking

More time with your puppy dog,
and his favorite squeaky toy
We're going on toy number nine,
but still I say "good boy!"

My life is full of blessings, these are just a few
Another special blessing is the friend I have in you!

So for today just let me say I truly wish you more
Of every blessing we share in life
from the cradle to heaven's door

If I Could Touch Your Robe

In my sorrow oh how I seek
Your glory and your hope
Guide my hand that I may reach
And humbly touch your robe.

Your word has taught you're with me now
You share my darkest day
My God, my Lord, my one true friend
Please hear me when I say,

If I could only touch your robe
God, listen to my plea
Without you I'm all alone,
My savior, come rescue me.

In the dark and bitter cold
A warm light I can see
My pain is gone, I feel Your touch
Your robe has covered me!

You've opened my eyes, I feel Your touch
I now realize dear God, how much
How much You paid to set me free
You gave Your robe and covered me!

Amen

To the Hero I Never Met

A soldier died for me today,
I did not know their name.
They gave their life unselfishly
so my life can stay the same.
Safe and sound I look around
to all God's given me
A price was paid for certain gifts
that I can't even see

God gave to me a soldier,
his life was not his own
He stood his ground protecting me,
when God, He called him home
So as I thank my God today
for this country in which I'm free
I say a special thank you for all who've died for me

And when I go to sleep tonight
in a bed that's safe and warm
Before I sleep I'll thank my God
for those in uniform
For a price was paid for certain gifts
that I can't even see
May I always remember the soldier
who gave his life for me

Lion and the Lamb

When the road you're on turns rocky
And life starts throwing you curves
Remember that every servant
Is no greater than the master he serves

When your life is no bed of roses
Remember He wore the thorns
We all have times of sadness
Every one of us mourns

When you feel lost and hurting
And your back is against the wall
One beautiful fact that is certain
One price was paid for all!

So if the day finds you crying
Remember His spirit is near
Never give up or quit trying
For He shall dry every tear

If the road you walk turns rocky
Think of the great I Am
Soon there will be love everlasting
When the lion lays down with the lamb!

Little Cowboy

I got a good hat, a nice pair of boots
and a coat for when it's cold!
Life is a joy for this little cowboy
and I'm only two years old!

I sit tall in the saddle with my grandad's help,
he helps me drive his tractor too,
I got the best grandad in the whole wide world,
there's nothing we can't do!

Life is good as we sit on the porch
and watch the sun go down
Then comes night with the stars shining bright
I'm the luckiest little cowboy around!

I got a good life, a great mom and dad
and a God for every season
My life is good in so many ways
and for oh so many reasons!

Live Every Day with Love

A day at a time I do just fine
These things are possible for you
So shake off the blues and lace up your shoes
Dreams can really come true

With sweat and desire
You rise a bit higher
The world is something to see!
With hope and with pride I find my stride
A new adventure for me!

If you know that you can or think that you can't
The truth is you're right either way
Nothing can stop the desire of a man
My desire leads me today

Live for today, today's all we've got
Reach for the heavens above!
Walk with me now, reach for my hand
And live every day with love

Lucky Me

I've got an old rabbit's foot
that my grandad gave to me…
At the top is a rusty chain
where I used to hang a key
That little key opened up a box
that held my worldly treasures
Rocks and coins and army men …
silly things that gave me pleasure!

I've got a worn-out bible
that Grandma gave to me
It tells me of a story of the Light
that sets us free
That Light it shines within me,
it's my heavenly treasure
Father, Son and Holy Ghost…
a Love we cannot measure

Amen

Mary's Lamb

Mary had a baby Lamb
whose fleece was white as snow
The Lamb became a sacrifice
for everyone I know
Who was and is, and is to come
as every knee shall bow
I wait for the Lion of Judah,
no greater one than thou!

To be first you must be last,
a beautiful mystery
Why oh why would my Creator die
to save a man like me?
Just as I am He sees my heart
and loves me anyway
He is the faithful shepherd
for all sheep gone astray!

So here I am on my knees
though some won't comprehend
When I feel lost and hurting
I go to my best friend
And as I rise to face the day
with everything I am
I thank my God I'm able to pray
to the Lion and the Lamb!

Meme

When I think of my grandma
her smile comes to mind
She had a beautiful soul,
gentle and kind

When I think of her home
I can still hear her say
Find some fresh air,
go out and play!
As a young boy,
my favorite place to go

The sunshine of summer
or winter's white snow
No matter the weather,
regardless of season
I loved her old house
and she was the reason

As I grew older,
doing things on my own
No more adventures at Grandma's old home
School, sports and dances,
homework and such
I did visit Grandma
but not nearly as much

Then off to college,
soon a wife and two kids
I often reflect on
the things that I did

I sit here thinking
how quickly life passes by
I think of my grandma
with a tear in my eye

My kids are both married,
they're all doing fine
They come home to visit
when they find the time

Speaking of visits,
if I had a wish of my own
I'd go back to see Grandma
at grandma's old home

My Christmas Gift

Soon it will be Christmas,
many gifts under the tree
There's no room for your present,
this certain gift from me
I took a piece of paper and found my favorite pen
The words I wrote are straight from my heart
It's my gift to you, my friend

If there's something you're really, really wanting
I couldn't guess it if I were to try
My gift is much more simple,
it's something you can't buy

And though your gift isn't under the tree
Nor wrapped with a ribbon or bow
Its beauty is the person I see
The care and the love that you show

I offer my gift as I think about you
None better could there be
Because of you I'm blessed, dear friend
And that's a gift for me!

My Dream

Last night I had a beautiful dream
I had wings and, yes, I could fly!
I flew up to the brightest star
And I took it from the sky.

I found you in our special place
Our secret with flowers and trees
I looked into your emerald eyes
As I got upon my knees.

I took your hand and gave you the star
Its beauty lit up your face
It was then you held me tightly
I felt the warmth of your embrace.

Tonight I'll have a beautiful dream
Full of secrets and stars in the sky
For you are what my dreams are made of
I'll love you till the day I die.

My Mama's Hands

My mama's hands used to hold me
When I felt alone and scared
It was her beautiful hands that showed me
How much she really cared.

When I think about my parents
My father was a very strong man
Yet he always said he felt stronger
When he would hold my mama's hand.

My mama's hands used to hug me
If I hadn't seen her in a while
She would wave at me when I was leaving
That always made me smile!

Angels have welcomed my mom for now
I miss her so very much
I miss the love in my mother's hands
Her warm and assuring touch.

Someday I'm going to Heaven
It will be a beautiful sunny day
I know her hands will guide me
If I ever lose my way.

And when I set foot in paradise
This humble sinner that I am
All my tears will be wiped away
With the touch of my mama's hand.

My Pretty Little Tree

My pretty little tree
with plain and simple lights
You can see it from my window
on this cold December night

Really nothing fancy,
no silver tinsel or stunning bows
My modest little tree could win
no Christmas shows

And though I own no trophy
for an elaborate display
Its ambiance can't be bought,
no money could you pay

A tree that lights up my house
with its simplicity
Brings a glow into my heart,
a glow for all to see

And so I keep it simple
for that very reason
My beautiful little tree
for this wonderful Christmas season

My Prayer

Dear God, grant me wisdom to know what to say
As I come to You now, as I kneel down and pray
Lead me by Your spirit as I come to You now
Lord, search my heart, some way...somehow

Know that my words, that my plea is sincere
Lord grant me Your courage, remove all my fear
Dear God, take my heart and make it brand new
For I'm just a sinner, I'm depending on You

Sweet Shepherd above, please look past my shame
I'm here on this earth yet I know Your name
Show me Your mercy, give me Your grace
For someday, my Savior, we will meet face to face

Dear God up in heaven, You seem far away
Do you know that I seek You, can You hear what I
say?
So if You are listening from Your throne up above
I pray, dear sweet Jesus, show me Your love

Amen

My Story

I've sat on many bar stools,
today I sit on a pew.
That stool led to a jail cell,
today I'm something new.
Here I've never been asked to walk a line
or blow in a device,
The choir's music sounds beautiful
and the people 'round me smell nice!
No one has thrown a punch at me
for something stupid I've said.
People get on their knees
and pray with me instead.
I still remember the bar stool
and all its misery,
so I choose to sit in a church today,
today my spirit is free.

Amen

Never Look Back

Keep moving along whatever you start
Main thing is never look back
Regrets often come but follow your heart
With it there's nothing you lack

The road you are on will get rocky at times
It's nothing to fear or to dread
Know in your heart that everything's fine
To doubt is just in your head

So keep your hands on the plow
Never look back, give all you've got for today
Wipe the sweat off your brow, but never look back
You're not headed that way!

Oh Breath of God

Breathe on me, oh breath of God
Strengthen my feeble soul
Let me feel Your presence
Oh God please take control
Fill this empty soul within me
So I may live forever
Open my eyes to things that matter
Strengthen my every endeavor
Breathe within me compassion
Your guidance I do yearn
In every form and fashion
Let no stone be left unturned
Breathe on me, oh breath of God
That I may clearly see
And give my love to fellow men
The way that You love me

Amen

On My Knees

My two knees and a bible, what else can I say?
For it's on my knees I show reverence
as I bow down to pray
And oh, such sweet surrender, if I'll only take a look
His mercy and grace and eternal love,
are written in this book

My old knees are worn out,
they hurt me some of the time
Yet when I kneel down to worship,
they seem to feel just fine!
As I go to the Father in secret
and I meditate on His word
My troubles, they all fade away,
my spirit soars just like a bird!

So as I read my Bible, I know
that everything will be okay
When my knees have walked their final mile,
the Lord will carry me on that day
On the glorious day when I fly away,
Oh how my spirit will soar!
The bible has told me where I'm going,
and I'll need my knees no more!

Amen

Special Holiday

On this special holiday,
we wanted to take the time to say,
From our house to yours we pray you are blessed.
For your family and friends we wish all the best!
And as you sit down for your holiday meal,
May every little thing be perfectly ideal!
Be warm and happy in a wonderful place
I hope there's a smile on everybody's face!
Great friends, loving family, plenty of food
And the greatest of all blessings…
Gratitude!

Happy Holidays from my family to yours!

One Foot in Front of the Other!

I remember these precious words
From my beautiful smiling mother
"Son, be strong and face your fears,
It's one foot in front of the other!"
Years go by and my mom is gone,
Sometimes it's hard without her
This road is long but I carry on
And I often think about her
For the words she said fill my head
With strength and understanding
I can face the world today
And today might be demanding!
So I lace 'em up, these shoes of mine
It's one foot in front of the other
When the world gets rough
And things get tough
I think of my beautiful smiling mother!

Smile and seize the day!

Open My Eyes, Dear God

Wisdom I seek, if just for today
So many things I've squandered away
Lord take from me now, this worldly view
Help me, oh God, to focus on You

Treasures on earth are fine some will say
Yet it was told long ago this world passes away
So walk with me, Master, as I reach for Your hand
Please open my eyes so that I understand

Open my eyes, for a moment to see
Whisper Your secrets that are meant just for me
God, only You know what I'm longing for
Please open my eyes, that I see just once more!

OPEN my eyes, oh precious God, that I may truly see
Guide me on my journey and open my eyes for me
Precious Lamb that died for me, restore me once
again
Renew my mind, for it's You I seek, open my eyes,

Amen

This World of Ours

Our world was once a beautiful place
We fellowshipped with God's embrace
Yet all, like sheep, did go astray
Our perfect order then went away

The unseen sculptor still loved us so
He did not leave, He did not go
Into the world He sent His son
For you, for me, for everyone

Oh precious Lamb that came to save
We challenged Him, we chose the grave
Forgive me Lord, what did I do?
My lust, my sins, my worldly view

Our world is such a beautiful place
For God has shown His perfect grace
He paid the price for all, you see
Eternal love for you and me!

Amen

She's Waiting for Me

I'm honoring myself more today,
so I start the morning with prayers!
And as the sun rises there's little surprises
like you standing at the top of the stairs…
Baggy pajamas, hair all a mess
and as you wipe the sleep from your eyes,
It's beauty I see and though you might not agree…
My prayers have been realized!
I head for the door, I tell you I love you,
I'm off to seize the day!
I'm grateful in spirit, you've strengthened my soul
There's nothing more to say!
We've been through a lot, the good and the bad,
I wouldn't trade for a single thing.
My dream, my darling, my love is unending,
That's why you wear my ring
I face the day, whatever may come
For I know I'm never alone
I'm blessed beyond measure,
for you're God's given treasure
It's you who's waiting at home!

Summer Rain

When my soul feels empty,
I long for just your touch
An oh so simple gesture,
yet to me it means so much
I need you here beside me
Promise you'll always stay
For in that vow I find my strength,
my troubles are washed away

If I could be a river with rapids to comprehend
My source of strength would come from you,
my love, my dearest friend
And if I am a river,
you are my summer rain
You fill me to my essence,
you ease my drought and pain

With you I am strong again,
you touch me to my soul
The rain and river are best of friends,
you make my waters roll
So when the sky looks troubled,
with dark clouds oh so near
I know I need not worry
for you will soon be here

Success

Everybody wants to be successful
until they see what it actually takes
Fatigue makes cowards of us all
and spirits eventually break

Walking along a lonely road
that many refuse to start
If only we knew a secret that's true,
starting is the hardest part

A burning desire, a will to succeed
that comes from your spirit within
To do what's required, to sweat and to bleed
with no other choice than to win

Rise up today, let go of your fears,
follow the want of your soul
Soon you will find with effort and time,
the treasure of reaching your goal

Soul and Spirit

I look for that freedom,
that feeling on high
Take all this sorrow,
these tears that I cry

Restore me to peace now
Please take all my pain
Just do this this one time
And I won't ask again

For I look for that freedom
The freedom to smile
For I'm worn down and weary
I've been traveling for miles

We're all on this journey
But I long for its end
Don't get me wrong, now
You've been a good friend

I long for that freedom
I search for the key
I know there's an answer
For both you and me

Just for today now
Let me rest and be still
For I know I'll do better
And I promise I will

I long for that freedom
It's hard to explain
Just do this this one time
And though I might ask again…

Amen

Still Searching

My darkest night I searched for You,
I sought You my saddest day
Pride and lust just won't turn loose,
silly dreams get in the way
We choose most of our misery,
so hard to let things go
For all my years I'm foolish still,
but one thing I surely know

I know how much You love me,
at least I hope I do
You're always thinking of me
and all of mankind too
Your mighty kingdom is in the heavens,
so very far away
Yet Your love embraces me,
if I take the time to pray

Consider me, my dear sweet Lord,
test my broken heart
Help me stand complete in You,
each and every part
"Well done, faithful servant,"
I long to hear you say
For my darkest night I searched for You,
I sought You my saddest day

Yearly Reflection

Taking time to look back on the year
A new one about to begin
Thinking of people, places and things
What a wonderful year it has been!

Remembering the times that weren't so great
Things always seem to turn around
Having you there, helping me up
When I was hurting and down

All the great moments with family and friends
Memories of seeing you smile
This, I pray, as the new year begins
Making my life worthwhile

Closing the year with positive thoughts
Ready to start a new
Thinking of people, places and things
Especially thinking of you

Happy New Year

That's My Puppy Crossing that Rainbow!

My dog used to chase butterflies,
he was just a pup back then.
I wish for a moment I could go back
and watch him be a puppy again!
He loved to ride in my pickup truck,
if I would just open the door.
I wish for a moment I could go back
and open up my truck once more!
If I could do it over I would pet him more,
I'd throw a tennis ball till my arm was sore.
I would sneak him a treat
when my wife wasn't looking,
I'd give him a big bite
of whatever she was cooking!
My heart really aches
for I've lost a best friend
But I know someday I'll see him again
Right now he's in Heaven chasing butterflies
One thing of I'm certain is that love never dies
I love him, I miss him, that's all I need to say
Until we meet again on that glorious day,

Every dog we have ever had has given us joy.
We are blessed.

The Art of Letting Go

Every little bunny
will someday hop away
I have no words of comfort,
there's nothing I can say

Every little birdie
will fly its nest of straw
There can be no exception,
for it's unwritten law

Surely as the morning comes
and the sun lights up the sky
To every bird and bunny
we must say goodbye

So for today be sure and say,
"I love you, don't you know!"
And always hold them near to you
For there's an art to letting go.

The Best Mom in The World

You're the best mom in the whole wide world,
I say this because it's true!
And of all the things that make up my life,
A special part is you!
So let me say this,
Because I want you to know...
You're truly like no other,
Thank you for being the person I love,
Thank you for being my mother!

The Weight

I bow my head down to pray a bit longer.
Slowly, so slowly my faith becomes stronger.
The Lord speaks to me, yet no words do I hear.
No words are needed, the Holy Spirit is near.
My soul, it cries out as God hears my plea:
"Lord, how can I carry the weight placed upon me?"
He gently answers, "What did the cross weigh?
How far could you carry on your strongest of day?"
Christ drank of this cup and was willing to die,
Would you be able or at least willing to try?
He died for the world, for all of mankind,
Taking our sins, He took yours, He took mine!
May the weight we all carry be lighter today.
Let us take one more step as Christ shows us the way.
I lift my head up for my burdens are gone!
May our strength be in Christ as we all carry on!

Amen

The Lights of Home

Lately my heart,
it doesn't feel like mine
It's like God has touched it
for just a moment in time
Somehow my heart,
it doesn't feel like my own
It's been given a secret
from God on His throne

My heart doesn't feel
like mine any longer
Somehow it's grown,
it beats a bit stronger
Lately the blood that flows
thru my veins
Has opened my eyes
and a vision remains

The lights of home,
in the distance glowing
My footsteps guided
by a force all-knowing
Away from many things
I've always desired,
Things that run you down,
wear you out, make you tired

One fine day it's gonna be,
all these things will turn to dust
The lights of home will be brighter then,
for every one of us
There's a mansion made for you and me,
it's built upon a mountain
For all who drink from the water of life,
an ever-flowing fountain

And for those who thirst remember this,
you'll never thirst again
For God has prepared a place for all,
away from this world of sin
So I follow my heart that's guiding me,
to the light upon that hill
The light is Christ who patiently waits,
He's waiting for us still

Amen

The Love Letter

Last evening as it was winding down
to the end of a peaceful day
I was thinking of a person I know,
trying to find their way
So I decided to write a letter
and send it to my friend
Lord, I've got this piece of paper,
I pray you'll be my pen

I wanted to share my life story,
such a mess I used to be
My middle name was trouble,
the black sheep of my family
Then the good shepherd found me,
He rescued a lost little lamb
I prayed when my friend read my letter,
they would know how grateful I am!

I prayed my friend's eyes would be opened,
to hear the Master gently calling
I wanted them to find unbelievable peace,
no matter how far they had fallen
Yet the more I read the words that I wrote,
my letter just wasn't right
I decided to thank God anyway
and I turned in for the night

Early this morning I opened my eyes
and there by the letter on the table
I paid no attention the night before,
but right there I had placed my bible
I then realized the note I had planned
had long ago been written
In wonderful words this perfect letter
shares how we're all forgiven

Later I sent my friend a gift,
the gift of God's precious word
I included a note that simply read,
in case you haven't heard,
I know someone who loves you,
His love is steadfast and true
I'm sending you His letter,
God's love letter to you

Amen

The Widow's Offering

Two tiny meager coins, it was all she possessed.
The rich having wealth of plenty
And when they all left, the widow left first,
for she was blessed among many
The rich people threw in large amounts,
Their sources would never run dry
A poor widow gave up everything she had,
Her Savior to glorify!
Two tiny copper coins, it was all she possessed
She gave after hearing God's call
The wealthy had given but a little,
The woman had tithed above all
When I think of the widow's offering
She gave, despite her loss
She thought only of her Savior
One who would die on Calvary's cross
God needs not one dollar bill
Nor one silver coin in change
Creator of the heavens and all the earth
The ruler over all these things
Even the widow's offering
Can't compare, or even begin
To equal what our precious Savior gave
To save the world from sin
The widow gave up what she had
There's a blessing in this story

For she is with the Savior now
Praise God in all His glory

Amen

No Greater Pain

There is no pain such as our Christ endured
And if you're hurting then rest assured
Pain and sorrow shall pass some day
Every tear will be wiped away

There is no sorrow like Jesus knew
For His last breath He gave for you
His every promise is always kept
Let us remember that "Jesus wept"

Our Lamb of God, oh Cornerstone
Beside still waters we're not alone
His rod and staff will comfort you
His love is timeless and always new

Let us rejoice for we are saved
Though the road is rocky and not always paved
An uphill climb it often seems
Take heart, dear friends, for we are redeemed

So take my hand and let us pray
And lift our voices somehow, some way
For all are blessed, Your chosen ones
In the name of Jesus, Your given Son

Amen

There's a Light Up Ahead

Even the darkest day
won't be here to stay
For there's a light up ahead
For every doubt and fear
a solution is always near,
There's a light up ahead
In the distance it shines bright
as morning breaks the night,
A beautiful light up ahead
With radiant persuasion
you can rise to any occasion
Always stand your ground
for things will come around
There's a light up ahead!

These Hands of Mine

My first bike, its handlebars
The keys Dad gave me to my first car
That special trophy for finishing the race
My grandkids' shoes I've helped to lace

These hands have held so many things
The woman I love who wears my ring
My precious children whom I adore
I've held them all and so much more

I've held this bible that I call mine
It holds God's word 'til the end of time
These hands will close one final day
And yet, even then, His words shall stay

As I reflect on all I've touched
All precious things that mean so much
They've touched joy and sorrow throughout the years
They've shaken with laughter, and wiped away tears

These hands are weathered today you see
Not quite as steady as they used to be
One day I'll have hands that are strong again
For I know Christ and He's my friend

My God is the Potter of these hands of clay
He'll take his vessel home one day
And as I'm led to the Promised Land
What joy to hold my Savior's hand

Amen

Tough Times

This is for a friend of mine
who's in a tough place today
Sometimes there just are no words,
there is nothing one can say
It's times like these, I get on my knees,
I say a little prayer
Thank you, God, for listening,
I know how much You care
Please give them strength just for today,
let them hope for a better tomorrow
Take away their darkness,
comfort them in all their sorrow
May they trust in You with all their heart
as they try to rise above
I ask these things in Jesus' name,
I ask these things in love
Thank You, Lord for hearing me,
thank You for this day
For You are the one and only thing
to help them find their way

Amen

Things always get better, if we trust they will.

Tick Tock

My wife and I were talking
just the other day
Amazed we were how quickly
time does pass away
We shared a kiss as we reminisced
About things we did in the past
We couldn't help but smile about every mile
And how they traveled fast
So there we sat, as we had our chat
It was just us three
Time goes by so quickly,
there was a grandchild on her knee!
As the days turn into months
and then years go passing by
A loss for words, how I feel,
yet I will give it a try
Cherish every precious moment
Be thankful for what you've got,
Love your friends, your family and remember
the battles you've fought
Life's a test so do your best,
you are given today
Always remember how quickly
time does pass away

Valentine for Connie

When I think of my love,
Connie is in my mind.
She's warm, soft and gentle,
Did I mention she's one of a kind?

She's my very bestest friend
When I'm feeling low,
And when things are just peachy
She's the reason that it's so!

No flowers, chocolate, candy or such
Can tell her how I feel
So before I go to bed tonight
On my knees I'm gonna kneel

My prayer to God is simple
Thank You, Lord, for my wife
The greatest thing of all things good
The greatest blessing of my life

We Will Stand Before the King

We all will stand before our King one day
Every head bowed with nothing to say
Your name will be called to confess how you lived
Did you try to love others
or did you take more than give?
The deceit of the heart will no longer take hold
For we all stand at the Throne
and the truth will be told
Did you take time on earth to keep others in mind
Did you consider their worth,
were you thoughtful and kind?
Did you seek to be honest, was there sometimes a lie?
To be honest, I'm guilty but did I at least try?
Did you live life to the fullest,
were you faithful and true?
These are the questions, for me and for you!
When my name is called and it's my turn to speak
My soul it will tremble for I'm often times weak
You'll hear no excuses from my unsteady voice
For our God is a gentleman and He gave me a choice
This morning my prayer is simple and true
God help me to be a servant for you
Give me the strength to help those who are weak
Let me look upon others with a love that's unique
May I always remember we are never alone
These things I pray until I stand at the Throne

What Will I Think of Me

What will I think of me
on the day that I die?
Will faith in Christ give to me
the will to say goodbye?
Will I fight for one more breath
come my final day?
Can I hold onto the thought
every tear shall be wiped away?

All things will pass away,
oh so very fast
Will I remember to look at the sunrise,
for it could be my last.
Can I fall in love with the sunset,
at the end of this special day
What will I think of me when
this world has passed away?

Mistakes I've made along the way
are far too many to mention
To anyone I've ever hurt,
it was seldom my intention
If I could live all over again, I'd do better,
at least I'd try
What will I think of me
on the day that I die?

If today I pass away, I want you all to know
My life was blessed by knowing you,
I'm sad that I must go
I'll wait for you on the other side,
for now I say goodbye
I hope you smile as you think of me
on the glorious day I die

When My Light Grows Dim

There are times in life when my light grows dim
I search for His strength and reach out to Him
Yes, I'll shine again from another person's love
For He answers every cry from Heaven above

All of the age, we possess a spark
A glimmer of hope for souls gone dark
Just as the sun encourages the day
May we lift each other up by giving it away

Thank you, Lord, for the love of fellow man
When life is a struggle and we need a helping hand
May we always be humble as we are here
for one another
Thank you for the light and the love of my brother

Amen

When the Master Calls Me Home

I had a dream of my first day in Heaven,
the Master had called me home
I've never felt anything like His embrace,
or the love that I was shown
He held me like a long-lost friend
and wiped away every tear
I thought, "This can't be happening!
I can't believe I'm here!"

Suddenly I thought of those I'd left behind
and again I started to cry
Christ gently smiled and said,
"Hush now, my precious child,
They'll be here in the blink of an eye!

They still have work to do, but dear child,
your walk is done!
My precious and faithful servant,
oh what a race you have run!
For you stood beside Me,
you never denied Me,
"For many, you shared the good news!
Because of your faith, some who were lost,
They turned from their worldly views!"

And as I awoke I fell to my knees
I thanked God for the dream I was shown!
I long for the day, my first day in Heaven,
When the Master calls me home

When the Sun Refuses to Shine

We can sit in dark places
when the sun refuses to shine
Together we'll light up the tunnel,
things will be just fine

If you're feeling small, like nothing at all,
there's something I must do
With every tear I'll stay right here,
I'll sit in the darkness with you

Whatever happens I'm right here beside you,
your battle will be won
Before the dawn is our darkest hour,
we'll wait on the rays of the sun!

Nothing at all can take what we've got,
especially the friendship we've shared
I'll hold your hand, I'll never let go
and though our view is impaired

When dark and obscure, of this I am sure,
I'm your friend and you are mine,
We can sit in dark places
when the sun refuses to shine

Winter Wonderland

Beautiful boy waking up,
sleepy eyed and yawning

A winter playground says,
"Hello this cold and frosty morning!"

Now I feel just like a bear
so off I bravely go!

Thank you Jesus up above
for all the pretty snow

Thank you, God, for Christmas
and presents under the tree

My favorite gift, this wonderland
You created just for me !

Where the Moo-Cows Moo

Breathing air and open spaces
You'll find me there in grassy places
Wearin' overalls like workers do,
I love to hear the moo-cows moo!

Daddy works while I play
We feed the cattle a little hay
God has blessed us this Thanksgiving
Nothing's better than country living!

When I grow up to be a man
I'll give my dad a helping hand
I'll wait a bit for I'm only two
But I love to be where the moo-cows moo!

Isaiah 56:6-8

New International Version

We all, like sheep, have gone astray, each of us has turned to our own way; and the LORD has laid on him the iniquity of us all.

Reflection on Isaiah 56:6-8

All little lambs run to and fro, to slippery slopes,
dark valleys below.

Wild and wooly, we are, like sheep.
So as we sow, so shall we reap

Awake, dear brothers, to a brand-new day,
though each has turned to his own way

We left God's paths to follow our own,
rejected as rubble our Cornerstone

Look now and forever what God has done,
He has laid on Him, His precious son

Temptation, sin, all worldly lust,
the iniquity of all of us

I look in the mirror who do I see?
The worst of sinners staring back at me

My God sees more in my reflection,
to live as Christ and His affection

We all, like strays, have wandered in sin,
yet our Shepherd leads us home again

Praise you, Father, for all you've done,
forgiving us through Christ, Your only son

Amen

Wonderful World

Let the sun brighten up your day
with its beautiful light

May the moon guide you on your way
if traveling thru the night

Let the stars that fall catch your gaze
and fill your heart with wonder

Let your spirit be set ablaze
from lightning bolts and thunder

May your troubles be washed away
with the pouring rain

With a gentle breeze comes needed strength
to ease your worry and pain

Just be still and enjoy the thrill,
feel all of nature's glow

Let us start a new, me and you
In this wonderful world we know

Words I've Spoke in Anger

If words I've spoken in anger
were tattooed on my hands

Could I look in the eye of a stranger
and would they understand?

Would I feel shame and sorrow
wishing I'd worn some gloves?

Could filth and dirt be washed away
with another's love?

Everyone has a burden,
we all must carry a cross

One thing of I'm certain,
my dark side is my loss

Hungry, angry, lonely, tired,
emotions come my way

The key, I think, is acceptance
and to watch the words I say

For words I speak are how I feel
I know you understand

Thank God we have forgiveness
for the dark side of every man!

You're Not as Young as You Used to Be

You're not as young as you used to be
There is a little touch of gray
But without you there is no me
No happiness for my today

I see the clock upon my wall
The hands move a bit faster these days
Yet I know why as time passes by
I'm blessed in so many ways

The life I am living with you by my side
The love you have given, the things we have tried
And when I have fallen and my wits are at end
You've always been there, you are my very best friend

Come the four seasons, we're older today
I've got endless reasons so just let me say
You're not quite as young as when we first met
But your beauty is timeless, on that you can bet

Oh beautiful one, I must confess
Time keeps on ticking but yet nonetheless
There's nothing at all that I'd rather do
Than to love you today as I grow older with you

A Mother's Love

A mother loves her daughter and so it begins

A bond until death much deeper than friends

Daughter becomes a mother, it's all in God's plan

She'll never turn loose of her baby's sweet hand

Through good times and hard times a mother is there

Nothing can change the bond that they share

So daughter, tell your mother how much she means

The things she has done, the things she has seen

Tell her you love her, look into her face

For soon, very soon, you will take her place

A Pony Named Pretend

Riding the range
on a pony named Pretend
Where the sun never sets
and your horse is your best friend!
You don't have to reach the stirrups
to ride tall in the saddle
I'm the king of the cowboys
with imaginary cattle!

It's a beautiful place
with a big ol' open sky
I never have to nap
and I never ever cry
Me and Pretend have the world at our feet
The life of a cowboy is mighty, mighty sweet!

So giddyup, Pretend,
let's make it to my home
We've had a lot of fun
but my mom, she's all alone
I'm a sure 'nuff wrangler
and we'll ride again real soon
And even though you're my very best friend,
My mom, she hung the moon!

All People Have Wings

"What if I fall? Oh, but my darling, what if you fly?"
—Erin Hanson

Listen! Do you hear the wind call,
and are you willing to try?

All people have wings
that are made from intention,

So follow your dreams
and I also should mention...

Yes, you may fall back
down to the ground

The wind calls your name,
such a beautiful sound

Let go of all fears
and reach for the sky

All people have wings
if they are willing to try

As I Kneel Down

As I kneel down, worn out and bent
I come to You now, I long to repent
And though You are with me, I feel lost and alone
I'd give this all up, everything that I own

Just for a moment Your presence to feel
Give me that moment so what's broken may heal
For on my own I'm weary and done
So I come to You, Lord, by the love of Your son

And as I rise up my hope is restored
I'm lost without you, my Shepherd, my Lord
Let me rejoice, this shall I say
Lead me and guide me, show me Your way

Just for today take all that I am
Though I walk thru the valley, a lost little lamb
I come to still waters, green pastures ahead
Though I came to You empty, Your lamb is now fed!

Amen

Here for One Another

Once in a lifetime someone will come along
They make you feel awesome, tremendous and strong
Your reflection, once cloudy, now shines like the sun
All because of that person and what they have done

No way to repay this gift you receive
They show you how much they truly believe
Belief in one's heart, your purpose and drive
They show you the joy of really being alive

Soon, very soon you believe in you too!
The unique and amazing things that you do
Once in a lifetime you must give it away
Go find that person that needs you today!

Just Around the Corner,
I'm Waiting for You There

Just around the corner,
I'm waiting for you there
Nothing can come between us
or take the love we share
Stay on the path you're walking,
I'll see you very soon
Today I am your sunshine,
tonight your stars and moon

When you're sad and lonely
please know I'm with you still
I am that little birdy
perched on your windowsill
And when you plant some flowers
and smell the morning rain
Think of me for very soon
I'll see you once again!

Just around the corner,
I'm waiting for you there
Believe this to your very soul
for I do solemnly swear
Stay on the path you're walking,
I'll see you, yes I will!
For I have always loved you and I love you still

Loving Mothers Everywhere

Do your best, that's all you can do!
Teach your children to be honest and true.
Teach them to walk with faith from above.
Do your best, do it with love.

With each passing day, as you watch them grow.
Stand out of their way yet may they gently know
You've always been there, they were never alone
With love and with care, for they are your own!

Tell your lovelies there will come a day
A cold dark world will heavily weigh
A burdensome cross we all must shoulder
With it comes wisdom as we get older

Do your best, whatever life brings
March to your drum and may your heart sing
Reveal your spirit and beautiful soul
For you taught your children and that was your goal!

Playtime Freeway

I'm calling you, Mom, it's been one dilly of a day
I'm stuck in traffic on playtime freeway
My car overheated and traffic's a mess
Will I make it for naptime is anyone's guess

Don't worry, Mommy, I'll be okay
Just letting you know and, oh, by the way
I'm out here alone and it's bumper-to-bumper
We need to postpone Bambi and Thumper

What's that you say? I can't hear your voice,
I know it's past naptime but I have no choice
My cellphone is dying so I gotta go
Just one more quick thing because you need to know

I play really hard because that's what I do
But when I'm not playing I'm thinking of you
Yes, I'll be late, this traffic is slow
But as soon as I get there, to nap-time we go!

That Emptiness I Sometimes Feel

Have you ever had a lonely, empty space
right where your heart should be?
It happens to each and every person,
Sometimes that person is me.

May the light in all His eternal love,
 may the Lord in all His mercy and grace…
May our King pour out His spirit,
 and fill up that empty space.

One day closer to Jesus, every single day.
 In the blink of an eye we all shall die
And return to ashes and clay.
But oh what a wonderful beginning,
 for there really is no end.
For our God has infinite wisdom,
and Jesus is our friend.

And on that blessed day,
 when I lay this body down,
When I take my final earthly breath
 as my family gathers around.
That empty space I sometimes feel,
 that space will be filled with love
As my spirit is finally free to fly home
 A home with God above.

I'm Simply in Love

If you've got time, walk with me
We can take any path of your choice
And if you don't mind darling, talk with me,
For I love the sound of your voice

I'm in love with you, it's simple
I'm in love with you, it's true
I'm so in love with you, it's simple
I pray that you love me too

It makes no difference what direction we go
 It really doesn't matter how far
I'm really just wanting to have time with you
For I cherish everything that you are

I'm in love with you, it's simple
I'm in love with you, it's true
I'm in love with you ,it's so simple
I hope that you love me too

Someday we'll end our journey
Until then I'll keep you from harm
Yet when that day comes and I draw my last breath,
I pray that I die in your arms

I'm so in love with you... it's simple

A Self-Made Man

All my life I was a self-made man;
when others backed down,
I often took a stand.
The world was mine and I made it so,
today is different
and I thought you should know.
You see, I never caused trouble,
at least from my point of view,
but trouble seemed to find me,
there was nothing I could do.
Most of my life I thought
I never needed God,
God was for fanatics
and people that were odd
Most of my life I did fine on my own,
now things are different,
for my God is on the throne!
All my scars have a story,
I've walked a long road,
but the scars of my savior have paid
the debt I once owed.

And as I kneel down, today
I know how to stand,
for I reached out to God
and precious Christ took my hand.

Most of my life
I've been a lost little child,
Running in and out of trouble,
but mostly running wild.
Then the Master has found me,
He was always at my door,
and as He walks right here beside me,
I need ask for nothing more.
Looking back on the years
and all the things I have done,
I try to think of bragging rights,
can't come up with a single one.
I cast my eyes to Heaven,
way up toward the sky,
for one day you see,
He'll come for me,
He'll come for you and I

So now I live from day to day,
a humble, grateful man.
I share the gospel story,
every time I can.
I share with all who'll listen
and though I once was a broken man
If we just reach out to God,
precious Christ will take our hand!

Amen

My Last Drink

My very last drink I ever had
Whiskey straight-up, I believe
Thirty minutes past closing time
The bartender asked me to leave

Even though I am my father's son
He's confused by the things I do
I have to laugh to keep from crying
If dear papa only knew

If there really is a God of love
Full of mercy and grace
Won't He look down from heaven above
And take me out of this place

All of my bones are aching
There's a train wreck in my head
I can't stop my hands from shaking
God, please let me wake up dead

I had a vision, early the next morning
It came on sudden like, without warning
My life changed that very day
It changed for the better in a positive way

God took from me my selfish desire
I had run a hard race plumb down to the wire
My life isn't finished, I'm sober, I'm fine
I'm living my life, one day at a time!

ABOUT THE AUTHOR

Walker Stradley runs a small family farm and ranch business located between Seminole, Texas and Hobbs, New Mexico. He is a husband, father, grandfather and animal lover. Formerly as wild and reckless as a person could be, Walker experienced a moment of clarity in 1992 that saved him and began a process of inner transformation, allowing him to connect with his faith and love of life. Walker considers himself, and his search for happiness, works in progress.